First published in 2005 by
Franklin Watts
96 Leonard Street
London
EC2A 4XD

Franklin Watts Australia
45–51 Huntley Street
Alexandria
NSW 2015

A CIP catalogue record for this book is available
from the British Library.

ISBN 0 7496 6123 2 (hbk)
ISBN 0 7496 6129 1 (pbk)

Series Editor: Jackie Hamley
Series Advisors: Dr Barrie Wade, Dr Hilary Minns
Design: Peter Scoulding

Printed in Hong Kong / China

The Wrong Shirt

Written by
Karina Law

Illustrated by
Tim Archbold

W
FRANKLIN WATTS
LONDON•SYDNEY

Karina Law

"My washing machine is quite well behaved but, sometimes, it does like to eat my socks!"

Tim Archbold

"A clean shirt is very important to an artist. Where else do you wipe your hands?"

Harrison loved football.

He was in the school team.

Harrison looked great in his kit.

At least, he usually did.

But not today. Today Harrison's football shirt was pink.

It was as pink as his sister's ballet dress.

SOMEONE had left a red sock
in the washing machine.

"Disaster!" cried Harrison.

Dad washed the shirt again
with extra soap powder.

But the shirt was still pink.

Very pink!

Dad tried again. This time he pressed the EXTRA HOT button.

But the shirt was still pink –
and now it was too small.

At the football field, Harrison didn't want to take off his coat.

He knew everyone would laugh.

"You'd better sit on the bench today," Harrison's teacher said.

Harrison's team played well. But, at half time, nobody had scored.

In the second half, David fell.

He limped off the field crossly.

"Harrison!" yelled his teacher.

"We need you!"

As Harrison took off his coat,
he turned even more pink.
Almost as pink as his shirt.

The crowd laughed. The other team laughed. Even some of the teachers laughed.

Harrison didn't waste time.

While everyone laughed, he ran.

He raced past the giggling
defenders.

He flew towards the goal.
Harrison moved as gracefully
as a ballet dancer.

He kicked the ball
straight past
the keeper ...

... GOAL! Harrison scored the winning goal!

The pink shirt didn't matter now!

Notes for parents and teachers

READING CORNER has been structured to provide maximum support for new readers. The stories may be used by adults for sharing with young children. Primarily, however, the stories are designed for newly independent readers, whether they are reading these books in bed at night, or in the reading corner at school or in the library.

Starting to read alone can be a daunting prospect. READING CORNER helps by providing visual support and repeating words and phrases, while making reading enjoyable. These books will develop confidence in the new reader, and encourage a love of reading that will last a lifetime!

If you are reading this book with a child, here are a few tips:

1. Make reading fun! Choose a time to read when you and the child are relaxed and have time to share the story.

2. Encourage children to reread the story, and to retell the story in their own words, using the illustrations to remind them what has happened.

3. Give praise! Remember that small mistakes need not always be corrected.

READING CORNER covers three grades of early reading ability, with three levels at each grade. Each level has a certain number of words per story, indicated by the number of bars on the spine of the book, to allow you to choose the right book for a young reader:

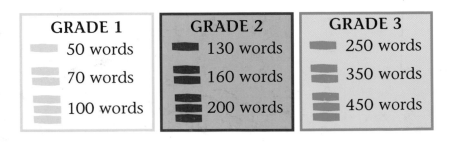

GRADE 1	GRADE 2	GRADE 3
50 words	130 words	250 words
70 words	160 words	350 words
100 words	200 words	450 words